LEHI'S FAMILE

Travels TO THE Promised Land

WRITTEN AND ILLUSTRATED BY

Robyn T. Pearson

Published by:

 JOSEPH SMITH®
FOUNDATION

Joseph Smith Foundation®
Salem, UT, USA

Library of Congress Control Number: 2020917907
ISBN: 978-1-64669-244-6

To Lee for his endless love and encouragement and to my 26 wonderful grandchildren that I hope will learn the stories in the Book of Mormon.

Nephi was happy that he had good parents. His father was a prophet, Lehi. His mother was Sariah. He had three older brothers, Laman, Lemuel, and Sam.

The Lord told Lehi that their city, Jerusalem, was going to be destroyed. Lehi was told to take his family and go into the wilderness. They left their home and lived in tents. They built an altar and gave thanks to the Lord for saving them from the destruction of Jerusalem.

Laman and Lemuel were angry that their father had them leave their home. They wanted the gold and silver they had there. Lehi reminded them the Lord had told them to leave Jerusalem because it would be destroyed.

Nephi prayed and the Lord told him his father, Lehi, was speaking the truth. Nephi told this to Sam, and he believed Nephi. The Lord told Nephi that because he was faithful, he would be led to a land of promise, a special land.

—

1 NEPHI 1:1, 2:1-20

The Lord will bless you, too, if you follow his words!

The Promised Land

Lehi told Nephi that he had a dream. In the dream the Lord commanded him to send Nephi and his brothers back to Jerusalem.

They should go and get a record of the scriptures from a man named Laban. It was written on brass plates and it had a history of their family.

Nephi said he would go and do as the Lord commanded. He knew the Lord would help him get the record.

Nephi, Laman, Lemuel and Sam went back to Jerusalem. They tried to pay Laban for the plates, but he took their gold and silver and would not give them the plates. He tried to kill them. They ran out of the city and hid.

Nephi crept back into the city at night. He was led by the Lord and got the plates from Laban. They brought Laban's servant, Zoram, with them. Now they would have the scriptures on the brass plates to help them and their children.

—

1 NEPHI 3:1-27, 4:1-35

Aren't you glad you have the scriptures?

The Lord asked Lehi to send his sons again to Jerusalem. They went to see Lehi's friend, Ishmael. They told him the Lord had sent them to ask him and his family to come with them on their journey. The family included Ishmael and his wife, their daughters, their sons, and the son's families. Ishmael decided they should go with Nephi and his brothers.

As they traveled in the wilderness, Laman, Lemuel, Ishmael's sons and two of his daughters decided they did not want to go.

Nephi was disappointed in them. He told them to have faith and be obedient to the Lord. They were angry with Nephi. They tied him up with strong ropes. Nephi prayed and asked the Lord to help him get loose from the ropes. His prayer was answered. Nephi was freed from the ropes he stood up.

Laman and Lemuel repented and apologized for tying up Nephi. They all traveled to Lehi's tent. They offered sacrifice and burnt offerings. This is how they gave thanks to the Lord, because they lived the Law of Moses.

—

1 NEPHI 7

Do we remember to thank the Lord for all of our blessings?

One night Lehi had a wonderful dream. In the dream he saw a large field. Then he saw a beautiful tree with white fruit. The fruit was the whitest thing he had ever seen! He ate a piece of fruit. It was the sweetest fruit he had ever eaten! Eating the fruit filled him with great joy! It was the Tree of Life!

He saw an iron rod leading along a path to the tree. It was next to a river of filthy water. He wanted his family to eat the fruit. He called to them, and Sariah, Nephi and Sam came to him. They ate the fruit too. Laman and Lemuel didn't come to him.

Many people held onto the iron rod. They walked along the path to the tree and ate the fruit and were very happy.

Nephi said the tree that his father saw stands for the love of God. Because of His love, He sent His Son, Jesus, to save us! This is joyous! He said that the iron rod that leads to the tree is like the word of God.

If we follow the word of God, from the scriptures and the prophets, we can receive the love of God and live with Him again!

—

1 NEPHI 8

Wouldn't it be wonderful to taste the fruit of the tree?

Nephi was blessed with a wonderful vision. In his vision he saw his father's dream and was told what it meant. He also saw scenes from the life of the Savior, Jesus Christ.

He saw Mary holding the baby Jesus in her arms. Nephi was told that this was the Son of God.

He saw John the Baptist baptizing Jesus. After the baptism, the Holy Ghost came down from Heaven to Jesus in the form of a dove.

He saw Jesus teaching the people. He saw Jesus healing the sick.

Nephi was shown many important things about our Savior.

Nephi had great faith in the Lord. He was taught many things in this vision.

—

1 NEPHI 11

We can have faith in the Savior, like Nephi!

One morning, Lehi woke up and went to his tent door. On the ground he saw a very interesting round ball. It was made of fine brass. It was given to them by the Lord to direct them in the wilderness. It had pointers on it to show them the way they should go. It was called the Liahona.

The families began to travel again into the wilderness. They used their bows and arrows and stones and slings to get meat for food. They followed the directions of the Liahona. It led them to the best places to find food. Nephi went hunting and his strong steel bow broke. Laman and Lemuel were angry because they couldn't get any more food. The families were very hungry. They thought the Lord wasn't blessing them.

Nephi had faith. He made a bow and an arrow out of wood. Lehi humbly asked the Lord where Nephi should go to get food. The Lord said to look on the Liahona. Nephi followed the directions given on the Liahona. He found animals for food. The families were filled with joy when he brought back food.

—

1 NEPHI 16:10-32

We can be faithful and obedient like Nephi!

They continued traveling and came to the seashore. The Lord showed Nephi how to build a ship. Laman and Lemuel did not want to help build it. Nephi told them that the Lord had asked him to build the ship. After a lot of talking to them, they decided to help Nephi. He didn't build it the way other men were building ships. The way the Lord directed him to build the ship was better than any ship a man could build. Isn't that great?

After the ship was finished, Nephi said they must prepare fruit and meat and honey to take with them on the trip. They also took many kinds of seeds with them.

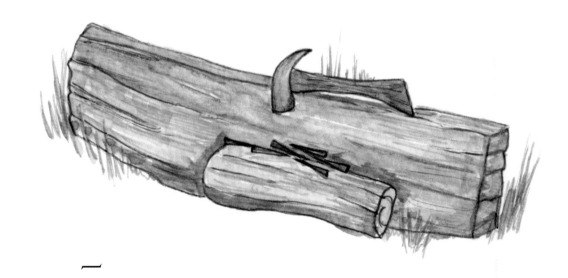

1 NEPHI 17:8-55, 18:1-6

We can follow the Lord's instructions like Nephi!

From the time Lehi's family left Jerusalem, to the time they sailed for the Promised Land, many years went by. Lehi had two more sons, Jacob and Joseph, as well as other daughters. Nephi and his brothers married Ishmael's daughters and they had children too.

When the family was prepared they entered the ship. Their trip across the sea began. The winds pushed them toward the Promised Land.

The Liahona showed them where to steer the ship. If they were righteous, the Liahona helped them.

Laman, Lemuel and some of Ishmael's family acted unrighteously. They became angry at Nephi and tied him with tight ropes. A great storm began. They didn't know where to steer the ship because the Liahona stopped working.

1 NEPHI 18:7-12

If we are righteous we can be guided by the Lord!

The storm became very bad and they were afraid. They knew the Lord was punishing them for what they did to Nephi.

They repented and let him go. The Liahona began to work. The storm stopped. Nephi guided the ship. After many days they arrived at the Promised Land.

—

1 NEPHI 18:13-22

It was a blessing that they arrived at their destination!

Lehi's family left the ship and went out on the land. They pitched their tents. They called it the Promised Land.

They tilled the earth and planted seeds. They planted all of the seeds in the ground that they brought from Jerusalem. The climate of the Promised Land was perfect for growing the seeds they had brought from Jerusalem. The seeds grew very well. They were greatly blessed by the Lord.

1 NEPHI 18:23-24

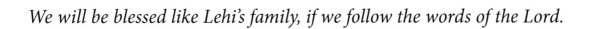

We will be blessed like Lehi's family, if we follow the words of the Lord.

They found animals in the forest. They found cows, oxen, donkeys, and horses. They found goats and all kinds of wild animals which were good for men to use.

They also found gold, silver, and copper.

The Lord told them they would be blessed in the Promised Land as long as they were faithful in keeping the commandments of God.

Elder L. Tom Perry, an apostle of the Lord, said the United States of America is the Promised Land that the Book of Mormon talks about (*Ensign*, December 2012).

1 NEPHI 18:25

This is where Lehi's family lived and many of us are blessed to live on this Promised Land!

GENESIS 49:22

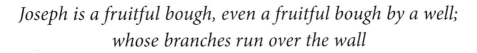

Joseph is a fruitful bough, even a fruitful bough by a well;
whose branches run over the wall

Each picture in the book is framed by a bough of an olive tree. This comes from the scripture in Genesis 49:22. "Joseph is a fruitful bough, even a fruitful bough by a well; whose branches run over the wall . . ."

This scripture has been interpreted to refer to the remnant of Joseph that sailed across the ocean to the promised land.

Also on each picture is a representation of the Savior watching over, guiding Lehi's family.

Robyn Temple Pearson grew up in Silver Spring, Maryland and has lived in Bear River City, Utah for many years. She and her husband, Lee, have 7 children and 26 grandchildren.